The Scottish Parliament
Charles Jencks

D0716849

There are two kinds of great public building: those like the new Guggenheim in Bilbao which are loved just when they are finished; and those, like the Eiffel Tower, which are hated momentarily before they are loved. Because great architecture inspires emotion, there is little middle ground, and many fine buildings have been aborted in their conception because a client has lost his nerve or the press has mounted a campaign to stop construction. In the new Scottish Parliament a risk-taking politician, and the leading client, Donald Dewar, held his nerve; and the architect, Enric Miralles, took as many design-risks as he could. The result is one of the most interesting, vilified, costly and marvellous buildings of our time. In time, like the Eiffel Tower, I believe it will come to be loved. Indeed there is evidence this process is already underway. But on the road to reaching this possible conclusion, one must understand its history and deeper meaning, and also the way contempt and derision have plagued the six years of its unfolding, just as fury marked the passing of the Old Scottish Parliament.

The main entrance to the Scottish Parliament building.

View of the Royal High School and Burns Monument, Edinburgh by Thomas Hamilton and David Roberts. Long a symbol of Scottish nationalism, the former home of the Royal High School at the foot of Calton Hill was a strong contender for the site of the Parliament and was refitted for this purpose in the 1970s. Protestors occupied a temporary cabin outside the High School for 1,980 consecutive days until devolution was agreed in 1997.

Unexpected benefits of Union

When the Act of Union was approved in Parliament House, Edinburgh, 1707, most Scots were suspicious, or actively against the construction of that new fangled piece of architecture called Great Britain. During the months up to the vote, mobs demonstrated against Union in Glasgow, Dumfries and Edinburgh. So great was their wrath that those politicians supporting the motion, such as the Marquis of Queensberry, had to be escorted to Parliament House every day, through the hail of stones and filth that was thrown at them. It is an irony worth savouring that the New Parliament has renewed Queensberry House, made it an integral part of the design and located there Donald Dewar's books and political memorabilia.

The story of Edinburgh's Age of Enlightenment, Scotland's great mercantile wealth in the eighteenth and nineteenth centuries, and the success of Scots worldwide following the Act of Union cannot be retold here, but it's important to understand the trade-off of money for nation that was made in 1707. Because Scotland had been virtually bankrupted by the Darien Scheme of 1698, was one-fifth the size of England and had no realistic economic future on its own, it was absorbed into the southern realm. Yet within 40 years Voltaire was to write, 'It is to Scotland that we look for our idea of civilisation'.

Nonetheless by the end of the nineteenth century Home Rule, devolution became a cause — the perplexing

◀ Queensberry House, re-harled and re-painted as an integral part of the new Parliament building.

◀ Nicholas de Gaudeville's image of the Scottish Parliament is the only known contemporary illustration of the old Parliament. Published in Paris in 1721, it depicts a scene from the 1680s: the Riding of Parliament, a formal procession of the King or his High Commissioner, together with the requisite nobles, burghers, commissioners and clergy, from the Palace of Holyrood House to Parliament House.

▲ The Stone of Scone, also known as the Stone of Destiny or 'Lia Fail', 'the speaking stone', which was removed to Westminster by King Edward the First in 1296 and returned to Scotland in 1996, when it was installed in Edinburgh Castle.

but difficult idea that there can be two parliaments with shared interests, such as defence, and mutual sympathies, such as a similar language. These interests in common would form a new type of independence that, like the new parliament building itself, has hardly been seen before. Two nations would co-exist within a single nation-state, the specific laws and balances between them to be worked out over time, and in fine print. They said it couldn't be done and, like another mad-construction, would fall apart into active warfare; either imperial slavery or total independence.

But a Home Rule movement did begin to emerge in the 1880s, a Scottish Office was set up in London and in 1885 the ancient office of the secretary for Scotland was revived. By World War I, the fledgling Labour party and Liberals took up the cause and it intermittently prospered for the rest of the century. Stepping-stones on this circuitous and bumpy path were the Home Rule Bill of 1924, Scottish and Nationalist parties forming in the 1930s, the National Covenant of 1949 (a deliberate echo of the same name of 1638) and the amusing emergence of a real piece of rock into the story, the Stone of Scone in 1950. In the early hours of Christmas Day that year, The Stone of Destiny was stolen from Westminster Abbey and its destiny was to end up four months later, deposited on the high altar of the ruined Arbroath

► The Scroll of Arbroath, a formal declaration of independence, drawn up in Arbroath Abbey, 16th April 1320.

Abbey, wrapped in the saltire flag of St Andrew. For Scotland, the symbolism of stones, the saltire cross and the famously democratic Declaration of Arbroath were once again wrapped into its history. The new Parliament building was to follow suit with its embedded stones and saltires in concrete, the cast outlines of the St. Andrew Cross, but a few more steps had to take place before the assembly became a reality. The Scottish National Party became a political force in the 1970s, a Constitutional Convention developed strength in the 1980s, the Stone of Scone was returned in 1996, and in 1997 the Labour party, which was committed by manifesto to devolution, won a landslide victory.

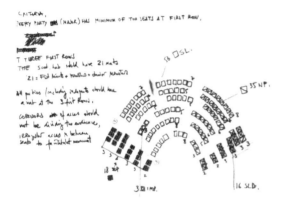

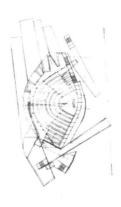

◀ Enric Miralles'
original sketches of
the seating.

▶ The entrance to
Queensberry House;
inscribed on the floor
is a translation from
St Paul in Scots, of
1 Corinthians,
Chapter 13, Verse 1.
Lettercut in steel and
whinstone, by Gary
Breeze.

On the 11th of September 1997, 74.3 percent of those who voted in the devolution referendum supported the re-establishment of the Scottish parliament. Thus Donald Dewar, the Secretary of State for Scotland, and the people of the country found themselves to be, somewhat surprisingly, in a new kind of nation. On 6 May, 1999 elections were held for 129 representatives and Labour and the Liberal Democrats won a majority

GIN I SPEAK WI THE TUNGS O MEN AN ANGELS BUT HAE NAE LUVE I MY HAIRT I M NO NANE BETTER NOR DUNNERIN BRESS OR A RINGING CYMBAL

of them: 37 percent of all Members were women.

Immediately, the architect got to work laying out a new form of seating plan – different from the Houses of Parliament – where opposing parties confront each other. In the Scottish version Miralles evolved a gentle, more convivial curve. It opens up the sides, so that conversation and consensus come before disagreement, at least architecturally. And Miralles provided each party

with seats in the front row, and movable seating, to follow the changes in political fortune. If ever an architect threw himself into the poetics of power it was this Barcelona designer, who gained inspiration from his home in Catalonia. This region, which has been trying to get out from underneath the yoke of Spain, has its own version of the Declaration of Arbroath and, like Scotland, is notable for its independent spirit.

Leaves and twigs win the competition

Enric Miralles won the commission for the parliament in July 1998 following an international 'designer' competition. From a field of seventy architects that competed, a short list of five were asked to provide conceptual proposals, rather than detailed designs. The Selection Panel, chaired by Donald Dewar, was unanimous in its decision that those concepts put forward by Enric Miralles and his EMBT/RMJM team were a clear winner. Most competitors produced a quick design sketch, to show the kind of style and solution they would adopt, while Miralles presented a more mystifying and poetic response. Significantly, the four other architects designed clear monumental assembly halls – circles and ovals – either placed on a plinth or set off against the city background. Their schemes were abstract and classical with modernist touches, and somewhat heavy. Donald Dewar, and the jury liked their monumentality less than the enigmatic gestures of the Catalan architect. Miralles showed a set of undecipherable images, a landscape of buildings, a tiny city as it were, nestling into the end of the Royal Mile. He summarised this image with an extraordinary metaphor. A set of green leaves was connected by twigs to that extraordinary rock outcrop known as Salisbury Crag, an extinct volcano.

Miralles' original twig and leaf sketches: the twigs extend out to the right, from the urban Canongate towards the Salisbury Crags (emphasised as a green U-shape in the plan, far right). The sketches also underline the design as a landscape scheme: sixty percent of the site is ground cover, forty percent building.

The Scottish Parliament as nestling green leaves? The press didn't buy it, any more than the visual metaphor of 'the upturned boats of Lindisfarne', but for Donald Dewar it was a clinching argument: "Miralles had ideas about how you put a building into the site that we found very sympathetic", Dewar told the press, "…he wasn't looking for a landmark building…he wasn't trying to build the highest tower in central Scotland as a mark of importance of the parliament."

As opposed to the classical monument, Miralles emphasised a nature symbolism connected to the landscape: "The Parliament sits in the land…Scotland is a land…The land itself will be a material, a physical building material…" Land, land, land – the phrase recurred like a litany in all his descriptions, and it is this that appealed to the jury. Ultimately the building became a kind of fragmented landscape, visually more a hard, fractal metaphor of Salisbury Crags than soft green leaves, and also an expression of what he called a "gathering place". This metaphor again struck the right note, and it became the title of the official BBC film on the project, a TV show that was itself destined

Rival competition proposals for the Scottish Parliament building.
◄ Elevation by Rafael Vinoly and Reiach & Hall, June 1998.
▶ Design by Michael Wilford Associates, June 1998.

to be part of yet another political storm.

As the building started construction in July 1999, it became clear that the initial cost provision which had been made public at the time of the designer competition was going to be inadequate. This provision had been based on assumptions about the project's size, function and complexity which were out of line with the proposals that the design team were developing in response to a changing brief. As this process of design development continued, so uncertainty increased about achieving key dates in the building programme and about the ultimate cost.

The cost of the proposal at June 1998 had been estimated at just over £62 million but this had been based on £27 million of risk being managed out as the design work proceeded. Concern increased about rising costs, and eventually in February 2000, an independent review was commissioned by the Scottish Parliamentary Corporate Body and undertaken by John Spencely, a past president of the Royal Incorporation of Architects in Scotland. This review placed a higher figure in the £200 million range because of the project's

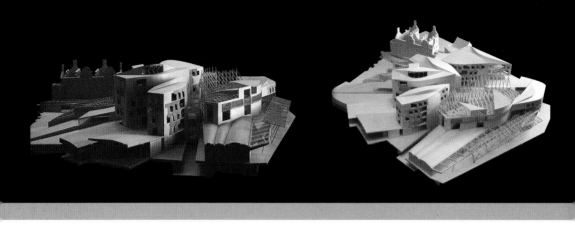

▲ Model rotated showing cutaway section of the debating chamber, above, and Queensberry House, Garden Lobby, opposite.

complexity and high finish. Although expensive, that amount would have been about average for such a new national parliament of importance.

Following a parliamentary debate in April 2000, a resolution was approved agreeing that the project should be progressed. In June 2000, a final scheme design was agreed between all parties with the objective of ensuring completion by end 2002 with construction costs estimated at £108 million within an overall budget of £195 million.

One of the problems that beset the building was poor communication between the two sides

of the winning team, the Barcelona studio of Enric Miralles and his wife, Benedetta Tagliabue, EMBT, and the Edinburgh firm RMJM, led by Brian Stewart and Michael Duncan. The working style of these designers differed radically, something that led in the beginning to various disputes including differences over fees. Happily, it also led in the end to an extraordinary mixture of inventive design and superb detailing, qualities that are rarely combined in one office. But what really threw the project on to the political burner was a human tragedy that gave the whole saga Shakespearean

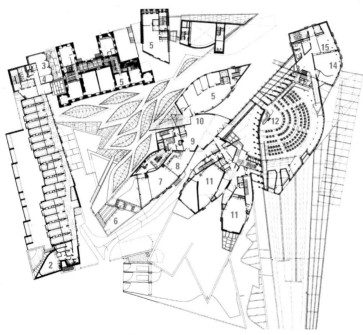

▸ Drawing at garden level illustrating
the public foyer and official entrance
from Canongate.

◂ Drawing showing access route and
debating chamber, first floor.

First floor, concourse
1. MSP offices
2. Fitness room
3. Party resource room
4. Meeting room
5. Office
6. Members' garden
7. Dining
8. Bar
9. Lounge
10. Concourse
11. Small committee room
12. Debating chamber
13. Commentary boxes
14. Press conference room
15. Broadcasting office

Site plan
1. Press tower
2. Debating chamber
3. Canongate tower
4. Tower 1
5. Tower 2
6. Tower 3
7. Tower 4
8. Garden Lobby
9. MSP wing
10. Queensberry House
11. Canongate

proportions; the death of the two protagonists, the only two who could have made an executive decision about the escalating costs, the architect and the leader of the client team, the former Scottish Secretary and now the First Minister of Scotland, Donald Dewar. Unexpectedly, Enric Miralles died of brain cancer in July 2000 and then equally suddenly, in October 2000, Dewar died of a brain haemorrhage, After these deaths, changes in design and cost-cutting became difficult, not to say impossible, since no one would admit to trimming the work of "a genius" and Scotland's premier statesman.

As cost escalation and programme slippage continued, the Auditor General for Scotland carried out an examination of the management of the project in September 2000 and eventually in June 2003, Lord Fraser was appointed to head an investigation into 'the whole lifespan of the project'. On 15 September 2004, he reported his findings and conclusions.

First, as we have seen, Donald Dewar and his advisors, particularly the civil servants mediating the figures, came up with a "wholly unrealistic budget". Fraser did clear Dewar of intentionally misleading MSPs over the cost, while he especially faulted the form of contract, "construction management", where the taxpayer was the ultimate client who had to pay for changes. Fraser said he found it "astonishing" that civil servants had not told ministers about the financial element of risk coming from "construction management" – and the MSPs didn't investigate at this point. Second, the politicians themselves expanded the brief considerably, adding more requirements and room to the original design. The area increased from 20,000m^2 to 30,000m^2, and the people to be accommodated from 300 to 1200.

Third, the terrorism of September 11th added £29.11 million to security changes, mostly in the form of blast walls protecting the MSP offices and the side facing Canongate. Here they also led, happily, to a very poetic incorporation of different Scottish rocks, as well

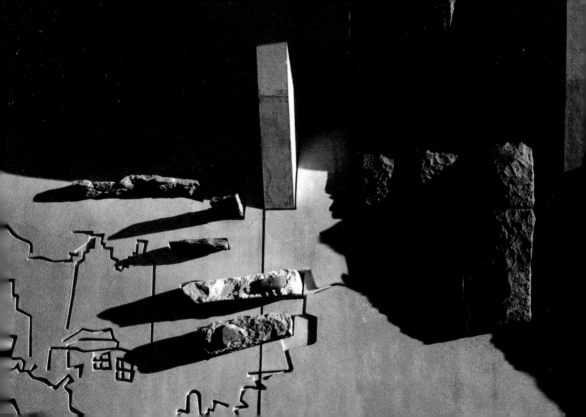

Aerial views of Holyrood, capturing the brilliant effect of sunlight on Miralles' leaf-forms.

as selected favourites of real Scottish poetry. Fourth, Enric Miralles' design was so complex, it was reported in the professional press that four out of five details had to be worked out on site; and while under construction, in response to client direction, he changed the shape of the debating chamber. Fifth, as mentioned, soon after the building started, the two protagonists who had most responsibility, died. Lastly, and returning to the first point, the implicit premise was that the best building must be built as quickly as possible, before it became a political headache. This combination of high quality and speed impacted upon cost and thus produced the official final estimated cost of £431 million.

Great expense thus became an integral part of the new Parliament's meaning; but to get perspective on this, one should compare it to other national landmarks, a special category of building. Richard Rogers designed the New Welsh Assembly in Cardiff, and ran into many of the problems faced in Edinburgh: political interference, cost overruns of about five times the initial budget, a hostile press, and long construction delays caused by management failure. He suffered the further ignominy of being fired for eighteen months and then re-hired. Norman Foster, who won a competition for the new German Reichstag in Berlin, had to change the design several times

because of political interference, and in the end took seven years to complete the scheme, way over the initial budget. Canberra's Parliament House in Australia, won in a competition by American architects Mitchell and Giurgola in 1979, was completed nine years later, and no surprise, at much greater price than envisaged. The 1960s EU Headquarters in Brussels not only took thirteen years to renovate, and cost hundreds of millions of dollars, but resulted in a pompous symbol of bureaucracy. The extreme example of time and cost overruns is the Houses of Parliament in London which took seventeen or ninety-three years to complete (depending on which architectural aspects one counts) and had all the usual troubles of political interference and price-fudging.

The conclusion is obvious. The new Scottish Parliament is about double the cost that would have been the most realistic estimate, of £200 million. Had this figure been agreed by July 1999, the Miralles' design would probably not have gone ahead. Contrary to prevailing opinion, the building was actually completed faster than other comparable national headquarters, in six years. Most importantly, it is a more creative and better-crafted parliament than its contemporary counterparts. For the last reasons, with time, it is destined to be loved.

Qualities of a national landmark

The new Parliament is, as mentioned, a tiny city with the high density and labyrinthine organisation of a metropolis. Like a city, it cannot be appreciated in one visit and like an urban district it must be contemplated from many angles. These vistas reveal a picturesque outline where two motifs dominate, the leaf-form and the black granite trigger-shape. The overall composition dances this way and that, like a city built over time and to no predetermined shape. The architects EMBT prided themselves on not drawing elevations, so what unity there is emerges from the layering of similar elements. To understand Miralles' architecture one must see his other buildings, which are equally woven together from diverse materials, the reverse of the Modernist doctrine 'less is more'. With him it is the usual post-modern riposte, 'more is different', a phrase borrowed from complexity science.

His method of photographing a site, based on David Hockney's collage of Polaroid images, also explains the notion of nestling into the urban and rural landscape. The Parliament building as a

Enric Miralles; collage, June 1998.

summation of layered details tying city to crag can be inferred by this staccato collage, as well as the idea that architecture can be made of ordinary related shapes given an extraordinary twist.

First are the diverse set of Scottish signs and images. Located just past the public entrance, and embedded in concrete vaults overhead, are versions of the traditional Saltire cross, but they are given slight tilts as are other signs cast throughout the scheme. Second are the forms variously called 'a hairdryer', 'trigger-panel' or 'tilted body.' This shape is most evident in the black granite elements attached to the façade, an ornamental motif that reminds many of a popular Scottish painting, the Reverend Robert Walker leaning forward on his ice-skates. This well-known icon, also admired by Miralles, is stylised and repeated in black and white and wooden panels that pepper the facades. Each one could be a statesman, perhaps skating over thin ice, but in any case it captures an image of well-balanced movement, a metaphor for democratic debate. They relate to the

other image of the human figure, the bottle-silhouette that lines one wall of the assembly chamber. Miralles was somewhat coy about these anthropomorphic shapes. He denied their existence and, when others pointed them out positively, he took the credit.

This allusiveness typifies the architecture. Local signs are incorporated into the design, but in a strange way. For instance, the crow-stepped gable, which one finds up and down the Royal Mile, is here

◀ "Bottle-men" in the debating chamber.
▶ Crow-stepped gable, Scottish Parliament building.

turned upside-down, and put under each window of an MSP office. Charles Rennie Mackintosh, an architect Miralles greatly admired, made the same humorous inversion of the crow-step, and if one is amused by such architectural inventions they can also be found in the garden-foyer skylights, again upside-down according to one reading. They penetrate into the space below!

It is, however, the vernacular and natural images of Scotland that are the most potent signs of nation-hood and the ones destined to become icons of the building. The hammer-beam structure of the 1639 Parliament is echoed and transformed in the structures of the Garden Lobby and the Debating Chamber. Embedded in parts of the Canongate Wall are different rocks, fragments of that geology which is Scottish destiny, and a detail that adds weight to this overall metaphor, the building either as a geological fragment or a giant Stone of Scone.

◀ The garden lobby.
▶ View of Queensberry
House from garden
lobby skylight.
▶ The grand stairway
to the debating
chamber.

Because the Parliament is low and complex, Donald Dewar and others felt it would never be summarised, as for instance the Sydney Opera House is, by a single iconic image. Yet in time, I believe, the complex will lodge in collective memory with the image that dominates the Garden Lobby: the curved vesica-shape. This, Miralles pointed out, relates to leaf-forms, and the upturned boats found on many Scottish shores, and a shoal of fish – all three. These petals swim, or float, or nestle according to prefer-

ence, over the Lobby, celebrating one of the great processional routes in contemporary architecture. Light spills down the sides of the skylights, a brilliant idea both literally and metaphorically, creating a general reflected glow that is without precedent. They pull you up the slight incline of a grand stairway towards the debating chamber, another leaf-form, and a giant one.

Here, the Scottish Parliament makes two important moves. Where the Houses of Parliament in London define democracy as a conflict of opposed

Above, hammer-beam roof of old 1639 Parliament, and right, drawing of new structure explaining how it works as a set of trusses that are cross-linked for stability, and thrusting upwards at one side, for light. Laminated and steel reinforced oak beams span the 30-metre space without columns. Left, the general golden hue is set off by the sparkle of lighting, cameras and steel nodes all arranged in serried ranks, an army of paparazzi and the eyes of the nation.

▶ The vesica-shaped
debating chamber.

elites confronting each other across two sides of a
chapel – so that truth emerges through disagreement
– the new parliament, as mentioned, stresses concili-
ation in its layout. The vesica-shaped debating chamber, with its gently sloping floor and the raked seats,
encourages consensual exchange, side to side as well
as head-on. You could be sitting in a lecture theatre
with very grand seats, widely spaced. The generous
mood is reinforced by the spiky dance of wood and
steel overhead, another version of the vesica-shape.
When debate becomes boring and pretentious, the
other MSPs and onlookers only have to look up and
stop listening to appreciate an interesting visual argument. How does this unusual structure hold the roof?

Here architecture is allowed to speak *le secret
professionnel*. Overhead is an airy truss with compression members in golden oak and tension members
in thin steel, but it jumps over the Presiding Officer's
head in the most unexpected way to turn into a vast
skylight, that pours a yellow ambience over the entire
room. That's worth deciphering, and so too are the

Exterior views of the Scottish Parliament with the Salisbury Crags in the background.

diagonal compression struts that keep the whole structure from collapsing sideways, like an accordion. Further interest is provided by the hundreds of hanging spot-lights and not a few TV cameras. These glistening elements define a space like the underside of a tree canopy. All of this engages the imagination, as predictable rhetoric drones on, refreshing the MSP for a creative rejoinder.

Even more unusual is the way light spills in from the sides. Whereas in the London Parliament debate

▲ Miralles' leaf-shapes realised.
▶ The grand stairway.

is closed off from the outside world, insulated as it were from reality, in Edinburgh the members are in visual contact with nature and geology, the deep metaphor that Scottish identity is wrapped up in its landscape.

This presence of glass everywhere is another striking aspect of the building and one that puts it squarely in the tradition of post-modernism, because it so clearly fragments the light and view. Post-Modern architecture is also ornamental, symbolic, related to history and complex spatially; but it has never been as labyrinthine as this. It takes four or five

◀ Flowing leaf-shapes;
aerial view of the
fifth façade.
▶ Committee room on
the top floor.

visits before one can remember the twists and turns
in route, the surprising way the vaults and structure
penetrate through the walls and spaces. There is
enough meat here for a ten-course dinner and several
PhD theses, and another good reason for not trying to
comprehend the scheme at one sitting. This richness,
reminiscent of the building type Miralles invoked –
the monastery – will pay more and more dividends
over the years as MSPs and their constituents wan-
der the corridors of power, and continue their horse-
trading. The amount of veiled lobbying space, little
nooks and crannies for an argument or a deal, is the
equivalent of back-street Edinburgh.

No smoke-filled-rooms are here, however, too
many surprising windows for that. The six committee
rooms, where decisions and policies are worked out

in detail, can be glimpsed from many angles. This is not the metaphor of surveillance and transparency, popular in Foster's Reichstag, but more one of connection and choice, seeing which debates one might want to enter and who is at them.

Every visitor will be impressed by the spatial virtuosity as indeed by the thoughtful detail. This last culminates in several places. First, following the monastic metaphor that underlies part of this complex, each MSP console-desk is a little pulpit in curved sycamore and oak. The Miralles motif of leaf and twig

◀ The debating chamber; MSP console-desks.
▶ MSP console-desks: Miralles' leaf and twig motif is echoed in carved sycamore and oak.

is echoed here, but it is the sumptuous carving and lamination that says very clearly Arts and Crafts, the Mackintosh and Gaudi connection that informs the entire building. Secondly, the individual MSP offices are rather cave-like spaces with dark vaults that have zigzags cast overhead in the concrete. These focus on an end-seat, no doubt the strangest inglenook in the history of architecture. Each representative sits in what has come to be known as a "Think Pod", and looks askance at a swooping curve located a few inches from the nose, or at the feet where there is a little "stairway to heaven" (on the exterior, those inverted crow-steps). A place for prayer, a cantilevered space-pod? Happily, the eyes are led by the trellis of oak poles towards the Salisbury Crags. In front of most windows, these reminders of twigs and leaves shield the MSP from the sun, and the inquisitive eyes of those inhabitants just across the street.

All this seems arbitrary at first, but as with much else it becomes more convincing on second glance. In effect, the inglenook focuses the seated politician on the line of rocks, looming out of the ground like some

◀ An imaginatively
   crafted inglenook.
▶ External view of an
   inglenook, veiled by
   Miralles' bamboo
   motif.

volcano-ridge on a walk. A spectacular cosmic view,
superior to Central Park in New York, it is the greatest
expression of raw nature to occupy the centre of a post-
industrial city. And this is why Miralles makes such a
thing of the inglenooks, with their sunshades of oak.
They are symbolic and performative. In effect, they are
meditation-caves, places for each MSP to gain courage
to act as an individual with a conscience, each one a
shrine to self-construction. Looking over the city and at
the Salisbury Crags, surrounded by carefully crafted
woodwork and elements that dovetail together like a
puzzle, the representative just might be inspired to rise
to the level of the detailing: complex, powerful, and
sometime heroic.

The windows of the MSP offices.

Stainless steel shimmers over the Committee Rooms, at the tower top.

New forms of democracy

Many people, when first confronted with the complexity and richness of this building, will be confused and annoyed. Modern and classical architecture are based on clear hierarchies, simple geometries, repetition and right angles. Post-Modern architecture, by contrast, is often ambiguous, curved, fractured and ordered by the addition of similar elements. Like growing nature it has a fractal order, shapes that are, in the language of geometers, "self-similar" rather than "self-same". Consider the twelve leaf-forms that nestle above the Garden Lobby. Like growing leaves each skylight is similar to, but slightly different from, all the others. They are also similar to the Debating Chamber to the east, and the four office towers that surround it – all versions of the vesica-shape. The towers hold committee rooms and briefing rooms of various size and shape, but they culminate at the top in large, oddly vaulted spaces. With their tilted skylight and reflected light, these committee rooms recall the religious architecture of Le Corbusier and the Baroque.

Then, to the west, is the undulating wall of stacked MSP offices, 108 cave-like spaces that stagger back and forth in sets. Again, the image and planning is more organic than classical or modern. Only Queensberry House to the North has a classical symmetry and layout. Being re-harled and repaired, its white surfaces are absorbed into the mostly white composition of the new parliament. In this sense, the basic eclecticism of Miralles' style includes even its opposite.

The most complex façade of all is the garden side of the MSP offices. Here the scale is broken down

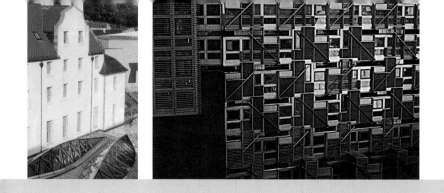

into the smallest fractal dimension as horizontal and vertical windows set up a staccato rhythm while giant drain-pipes play on the diagonal. There is nothing quite like it anywhere else, unless it is Miralles' own work in Utrecht and Barcelona where he developed many of the ideas. Again this façade reveals his notion that in a large building, the system should not dominate over the individual, that small scale is the right scale for democratic institutions.

But the way the building brings in the public and allows it to congregate in the streets and landscape around is an important innovation. Think back to "The Mother of All Parliaments", as Margaret Thatcher dubbed the Palace of Westminster, or forward from

there to Washington DC, and its government based on the Lockean balance of powers, the legislature, judiciary and executive branches. Recall how these institutional arrangements, and the buildings that house them, have grown from the medieval townships, and before that from the forum of Rome and the agora of Athens. What is strange about this history is that Anglo-Saxon politics has made an amazing invention – democracy without the people – that is, without a place for them to meet collectively and express themselves as a force. The English and then the Americans are suspicious of such congregations, worrying about mob behaviour and preferring the representation by atomised individuals. Hence, there are

no collective spaces for spontaneous gatherings and demonstrations. In England the public had to appropriate Trafalgar Square by force. In Washington DC, the civil rights movement of the 1960s did the same thing with the area outside Lincoln's Monument.

In Anglo-Saxon democracy, the public, when they do get a look-in, is fobbed off with a triangle of grass at Speaker's Corner, or left to a square they have to steal, a Royal Park or a Mall. Contrast this with European democracy, where there is a tradition of the square or piazza or French *place*, and one understands the arguments of Hannah Arendt. As she points out, the people have to hear themselves as an entity, see themselves speak and act as if in a collective mirror, in order to be a political force. If these spaces are provided, as they are in Europe, then as the examples of 1989 show, the people can gauge their own response to such events as an open-air lecture by Ceausescu (it brought him down), or an occupation of the main square in Prague (it led to the Velvet Revolution). This

The turfed vaults will grow wild, like the crags.

fundamental institutional space of democracy is provided at the Scottish Parliament, for the first time in recent Anglo-Saxon practice, by a European architect.

Miralles, the Catalan, has given a new twist to the continental idea of the agora, he has turned it into a soft, turfed place. Taking the same gentle curves that he uses on the debating chamber, he creates a shallow amphitheatre of steps and stairs and in this way sets up a clear equation between the people's debates and those of their representatives. In his early statements

the architect kept mentioning the land, and here following a trend of both the gardening world and architecture, he has created a landform of stepped contours. This long "tail" of the building, the twigs and stem of his original metaphor, connects the building to Salisbury Crags. Poetically it ties the "leaf fractals" of the structure to the rock fractals of the extinct volcano. In this way it also becomes the ancient memory of "the gathering place", the primitive democracy of clan elders meeting in the wild, an image that Miralles

Outdoor assembly area, a turfed agora for 10,000 to gather.

drew and words he put on a plan. In effect, this open agora contrasts with the other areas: the ceremonial entrance at the corner that is used on state occasions and the opening of parliament; Queensberry House used by officials; and the press and members' entrances.

The forms of democracy are spread out, there is no centre of power; as in Anglo-Saxon theory the process is one of competitive balance between interests. But here for a change citizens are given a place to hear themselves think, and see themselves react.

Behind this shallow theatre, the concrete vaults that greet the visitor at the entrance are covered in a bushy grass. They taper and thereby point toward the natural sculpture of the crag. Three reflecting pools, in distorted versions of the vesica-shape, remind one of the countless ponds that appear and disappear in Scotland.

In such ways, this building explores new territory for Scottish identity and for architecture. In the era of the iconic building, it creates an iconology of references to nature and the locale, using complex messages as a substitute for the one-liner. Instead of being a monumental building, as is the usual capital landmark, it nestles its way into the environment, an icon of organic resolution, of knitting together nature and culture into a complex union. It furthers the idea that Scottish identity is closely associated with the rugged landscape and urban experience in which it has grown.

Her Majesty the Queen opened
the new Scottish Parliament on
9th October 2004.

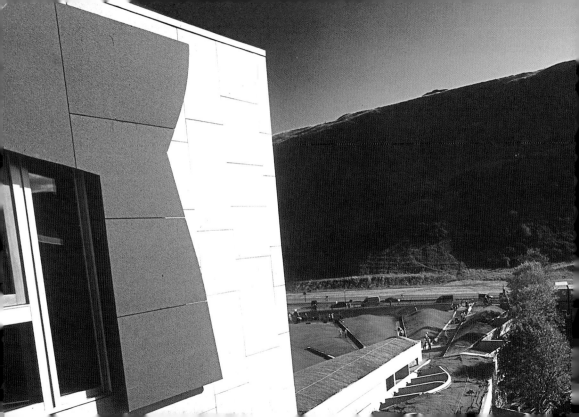

View from the Scottish Parliament towards Our Dynamic Earth and Salisbury Crags.

This edition copyright © Scala Publishers Ltd 2005
Text copyright © Charles Jencks 2005

First published in 2005 by:
Scala Publishers Ltd
Northburgh House
10 Northburgh Street
London EC1V 0AT
ISBN 1 85759 379 0

Designed by Anikst Design.
Edited by David Campbell, Oliver Craske, Katy Moran.

Printed in Spain.
10 9 8 7 6 5 4 3 2 1

Photography by Adam Elder. All images copyright © The Scottish Parliamentary Corporate Body except as follows:

5 (left), 30–31, 32, 35 (right), 45, 46, 48, 54 (right), 55, 56, 59, 62–63: Charles Jencks.
8: RoyalScottish Academy .
10 (left): © Crown Copyright reproduced courtesy of Historic Scotland.
10 (right): © The Trustees of the National Museums of Scotland.
11: National Archives of Scotland. By permission of the Keeper of the Records of Scotland (ref SP13/7).
18: Elevation by Rafael Vinoly and Reiach & Hall.
19: Design by Michael Wilford Associates.
26, 27: BBC Scotland.
35 (left): Andrew Wu.
37 (top): © The Gazetteer for Scotland (www.geo.ed.ac.uk/scotgaz).
60: Chris Furlong, Getty Images.

Charles Jencks's most recent book, *The Iconic Building*, will appear in April 2005.

◀ Front cover: The Scottish Parliament's leaf-shaped roofs.
▶ Back cover: Inside the debating chamber.